Little Dolphin

By Sue Unstead

LONDON, NEW YORK, MUNICH,
MELBOURNE, AND DELHI

DK LONDON
Series Editor Deborah Lock
Project Art Editor Hoa Luc
Producers, Pre-production
Francesca Wardell, Vikki Nousiainen
Illustrator Tim McDonagh

Reading Consultant
Shirley Bickler

DK DELHI
Editor Nandini Gupta
Assistant Art Editor Yamini Panwar
DTP Designers Anita Yadav, Mohammad Usman
Picture Researcher Deepak Negi
Deputy Managing Editor Soma B. Chowdhury

First published in Great Britain by
Dorling Kindersley Limited
80 Strand, London, WC2R 0RL

Printed and bound in China by South China Printing Company.

The publisher would like to thank the following for
their kind permission to reproduce their photographs:
(Key: a-above; b-below/bottom; c-centre; f-far; l-left; r-right; t-top)
14 Dorling Kindersley: Laszlo Veres (cl, crb). **15 Dorling Kindersley:** Laszlo Veres (tr, bl, cb).
24-25 Fotolia: StarJumper / Valeriy Kalyuzhnyy. **42 Getty Images:** Photodisc / Siede Preis (cl, clb).
43 Getty Images: Photodisc / Siede Preis (tl, cla, clb, bl)
Jacket images: Front cover: Corbis: age fotostock Spain S.L. / Fco. Javier Gutiérrez

All other images © Dorling Kindersley
For further information see: www.dkimages.com

Discover more at
www.dk.com

Contents

Rosie's Story

I am Rosie.
Have you ever seen
a dolphin leap right
out of the water?
Have you ever seen
a dolphin jump for joy?
Have you ever seen
a dolphin smile?
Well, I have!
Let me tell you
the story.

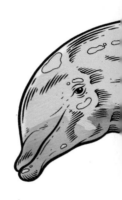

Chapter 1

Little Dolphin lives
in the sparkly blue sea.
As soon as he was born,
his Mama took him
up, up, up to snatch
his very first breath
of air.

Mama calls to Little Dolphin
all the time.
"Wheee, wheee!
Where are you?"

Little Dolphin calls back to her.
He has his own song,
"Wheee, whooooa!
Here I am, Mama."

Little Dolphin stays close
to his Mama.
She teaches him how to dive
and how to leap over
the waves.
But he longs to play with
the bigger dolphins.

"When can I join them?"
he asks.
"When you can swim fast,
Little Dolphin," says Mama.

Look at Me

1 beak
I have two rows of teeth perfect for grabbing slippery fish.

2 blowhole
I breathe out and I breathe in through this hole.

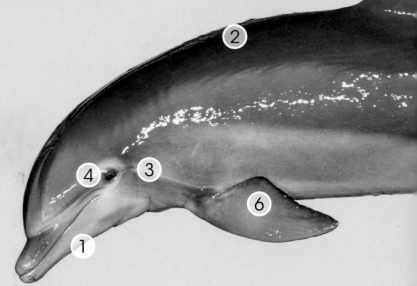

3 ear
I can hear very well under water.

4 eye
I can see under water.

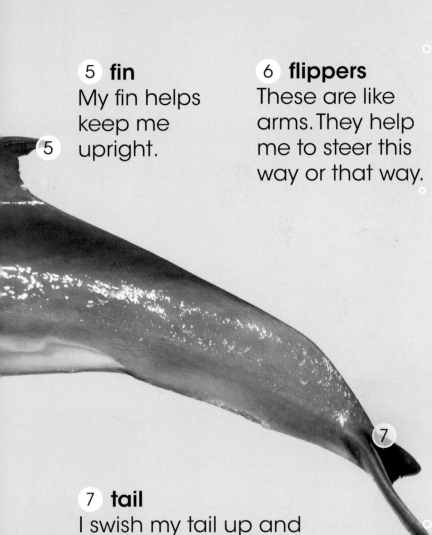

5 fin
My fin helps keep me upright.

6 flippers
These are like arms. They help me to steer this way or that way.

7 tail
I swish my tail up and down to swim fast. My sleek body helps me to slip through the water.

13

Who is Talking?

It is very noisy under the sea.
Dolphins chatter all the time.

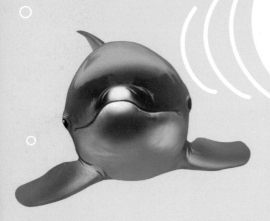

"Wheee, whooa! Hello. It is me and I am over here."

"Click-click-click-click. What is that over there?"

"Click-click-click-click. Watch out, sharks are about."

"Click-click-click-click," goes the dolphin. The sound ripples out in the water. It bounces back if there is something about. The sound helps the dolphin find fish.

15

Chapter 2

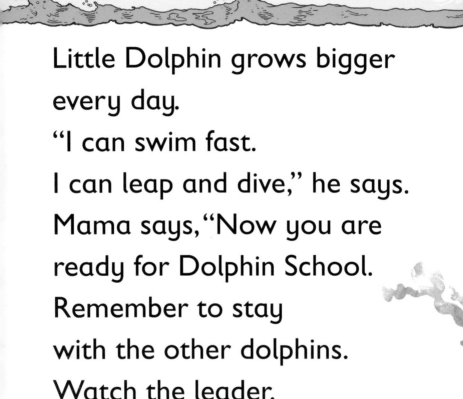

Little Dolphin grows bigger
every day.
"I can swim fast.
I can leap and dive," he says.
Mama says, "Now you are
ready for Dolphin School.
Remember to stay
with the other dolphins.
Watch the leader.
Look out for big boats."

Little Dolphin swims away
with a swish of his tail.
He joins the other dolphins.
They play follow the leader.
They play catch that fish.
They see who can jump
the highest.
"Wheee, wheeoa."
"Click-click-click."

Rrrr, rumble, rumble, rrrr.

"Listen! What is that sound?"
asks the biggest dolphin.

"A ship! It is a ship's engine,"
cries another dolphin.
"Quick! Let us chase it,"
says the biggest dolphin.

Food Chain

A food chain shows what feeds on what. Follow the arrows of the dolphin's food chain.

dolphin

shark

killer whale

Sun's heat (always begins a food chain)

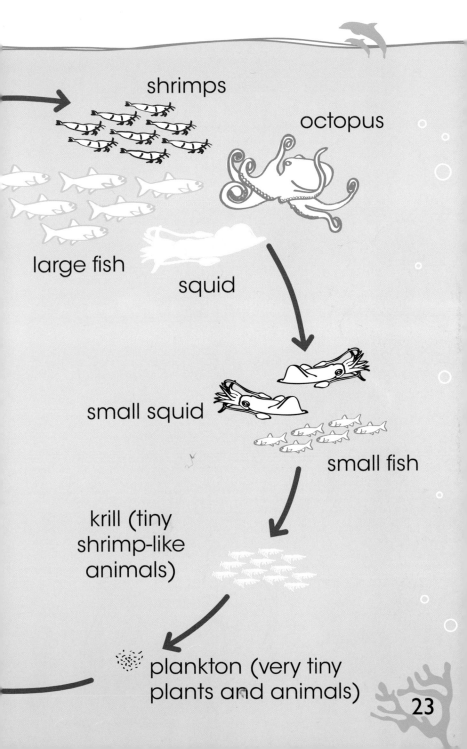

shrimps

octopus

large fish

squid

small squid

small fish

krill (tiny
shrimp-like
animals)

plankton (very tiny
plants and animals)

Dolphin Facts

Smart dolphins
Dolphins are clever
animals and love to play.

Friendly dolphins
They live in groups of
10 to12 dolphins called
pods, or schools.

Hold your breath
A dolphin usually comes up
to the surface for breath every
two minutes, but can hold
its breath for much longer.

Long life
A dolphin can live
for 25 years.

Jump for joy
A dolphin can leap up
out of water higher than
a double-decker bus.

Deep dives
A dolphin can dive deeper
than a 75-storey skyscraper
and hold its breath for more
than five minutes.

Baby dolphins
A young dolphin is called a calf.
Dolphin mothers have one calf
at a time. A calf stays with
its mother for 3 to 5 years.

Dolphin names
A female dolphin is
called a cow. A male
dolphin is called a bull.

Chapter 3

Here comes the ship!
A foamy wave pushes through
the water.
"Wheee!
Let us dive under it.
Whooah!
Let us jump in front of it,"
say the dolphins.

Splash! Splash!

"This is fun!" says Little Dolphin.

There is a dark shadow
above them.
Little Dolphin hears the thump
of the engine.
He feels the swoosh
from the propellers.
"Oooh! It is scary,"
thinks Little Dolphin.
He swims fast.

29

"Help! I cannot keep up,"
says Little Dolphin.
"The ship is too fast for me.
Where is everyone?
Click-click-click."

No-one answers.
Little Dolphin is alone.
"Wheee, whoa, Maaama!"
he cries.

Swimming Races

Dolphins can swim fast but they are not the fastest swimmers.

Number 1: sailfish   110 kph (68 mph)

Number 2: shark   53 kph (33 mph)

Number 3: dolphin

Number 4: Olympic swimmer

Number 5: goldfish

Speed guide
kph = kilometres per hour
mph = miles per hour

Whoosh! Super fast!

Very fast!

48 kph (30 mph)   Fast!

8 kph (5 mph)   Slow!

2 kph (1 mph)   Very slow!

Chapter 4

Whoosh!

Little Dolphin pops his head
out of the water.
"Look! There is a white sail.
It must be a boat.
I will follow you,"
thinks Little Dolphin.
A girl on board the boat
sees Little Dolphin.
The girl is called Rosie.

35

The fishing boat chugs back
to port.
Little Dolphin follows,
tired and lost.
"You must go back out
to sea," says Rosie.
She runs to fetch
her own small boat.
"I must save Little Dolphin,"
she thinks.

She remembers what her own
Mama told her when she was
a young girl.
"Stay with the school,
watch the leader and
look out for big boats,"
she thinks.

"Follow me, Little Dolphin,"
she calls.
Little Dolphin follows
her small boat.

Out in the bay, Little Dolphin hears his Mama calling, "Wheee, whee! Where are you?"

"Wheee, whooa!" he cries. "Here I am, Mama!"

Rosie sees two dolphins leaping.
She thinks they are smiling, too.
What a happy day!

Happy Families

Dolphins are related to other sea animals, like whales and porpoises. Meet some members of this family.

Bottlenose dolphins are playful and friendly. They love to jump and dive near boats. Often they swim near the coast.

Harbour porpoises are shy and only show a fin above the water. Sometimes they get trapped in fishing nets.

Spinner dolphins

are fast swimmers.
They twist and spin when
they leap out of the water.
They live in huge schools
of hundreds of dolphins.

River dolphins

live in the Amazon river.
They poke the mud with
that long nose to find fish
and crabs.

Killer whales

are the biggest dolphins
and are fierce hunters.
They live in big pods
of up to 150 whales.

Sperm whales

are giants. They dive to
the bottom of the ocean.
They can stay under
water for two hours.
They can live to 75 years
of age.

43

Little Dolphin Quiz

1. What does a dolphin use its flipper for?

2. What is a group of dolphins called?

3. What do the dolphins chase?

4. What is a baby dolphin called?

5. How long can a sperm whale live for?

Answers on page 48.

Glossary

Amazon long river in South America

beak mouth part of a dolphin used for grabbing food

blowhole hole on a dolphin's head used for breathing in and out

killer whale large black-and-white toothed whale

porpoise black toothed whale with a flat snout

port place for ships to load and unload

propeller blades that turn to make a boat move

Guide for Parents

DK Reads is a three-level interactive reading adventure series for children, developing the habit of reading widely for both pleasure and information. These chapter books have an exciting main narrative interspersed with a range of reading genres to suit your child's reading ability, as required by the National Curriculum. Each book is designed to develop your child's reading skills, fluency, grammar awareness, and comprehension in order to build confidence and engagement when reading.

Ready for a *Beginning to Read* book

YOUR CHILD SHOULD

- be using phonics, including consonant blends, such as bl, gl and sm, to read unfamiliar words; and common word endings, such as plurals, ing, ed and ly.
- be using the storyline, illustrations and the grammar of a sentence to check and correct his/her own reading.
- be pausing briefly at commas, and for longer at full stops; and altering his/her expression to respond to question, exclamation and speech marks.

A VALUABLE AND SHARED READING EXPERIENCE

For many children, reading requires much effort but adult participation can make this both fun and easier. So here are a few tips on how to use this book with your child.

TIP 1 Check out the contents together before your child begins:

- read the text about the book on the back cover.
- read through and discuss the contents page together to heighten your child's interest and expectation.
- make use of unfamiliar or difficult words on the page in a brief discussion.
- chat about the non-fiction reading features used in the book, such as headings, captions, recipes, lists or charts.

TIP 2 Support your child as he/she reads the story pages:

- give the book to your child to read and turn the pages.

- where necessary, encourage your child to break a word into syllables, sound out each one and then flow the syllables together. Ask him/her to reread the sentence to check the meaning.

- when there's a question mark or an exclamation mark, encourage your child to vary his/her voice as he/she reads the sentence. Demonstrate how to do this if it is helpful.

TIP 3 Praise, share and chat:

- the factual pages tend to be more difficult than the story pages, and are designed to be shared with your child.

- ask questions about the text and the meaning of the words used. These help to develop comprehension skills and awareness of the language used.

A FEW ADDITIONAL TIPS

- Try and read together everyday. Little and often is best. These books are divided into manageable chapters for one reading session. However after 10 minutes, only keep going if your child wants to read on.

- Always encourage your child to have a go at reading difficult words by themselves. Praise any self-corrections, for example, "I like the way you sounded out that word and then changed the way you said it, to make sense."

- Read other books of different types to your child just for enjoyment and information.

Series consultant **Shirley Bickler** is a longtime advocate of carefully crafted, enthralling texts for young readers. Her LIFT initiative for infant teaching was the model for the National Literacy Strategy Literacy Hour, and she is co-author of *Book Bands for Guided Reading* published by Reading Recovery based at the Institute of Education.

Index

Answers for the Little Dolphin Quiz:
1. Steering; **2.** A pod or school; **3.** A ship;
4. A calf; **5.** 75 years.